Weekly Reader Books presents

Thor Heyerdahl
Viking Scientist

by
Wyatt Blassingame

Elsevier/Nelson Books
New York

For
Curtis Blassingame

This book is a presentation of
WEEKLY READER BOOKS.

Weekly Reader Books offers book clubs for
children from preschool through junior high school.
All quality hardcover books are selected by
a distinguished Weekly Reader Selection Board.

For further information write to:
WEEKLY READER BOOKS
1250 Fairwood Ave.
Columbus, Ohio 43216

Library of Congress Cataloging in Publication Data

Blassingame, Wyatt.
   Thor Heyerdahl, Viking scientist.

   Includes index.
   1. Heyerdahl, Thor—Juvenile literature.   2. Ex-
plorers—Norway—Biography—Juvenile literature.
I. Title
G306.H47B57   1979   910′.92′4 [B]   79–1002
ISBN 0–525–66626–5

Published in the United States by Elsevier/Nelson Books, a division
of Elsevier-Dutton Publishing Company, Inc., New York. Published simultaneously in Don Mills, Ontario, by Thomas Nelson
and Sons (Canada) Limited. Printed in the U.S.A.

Contents

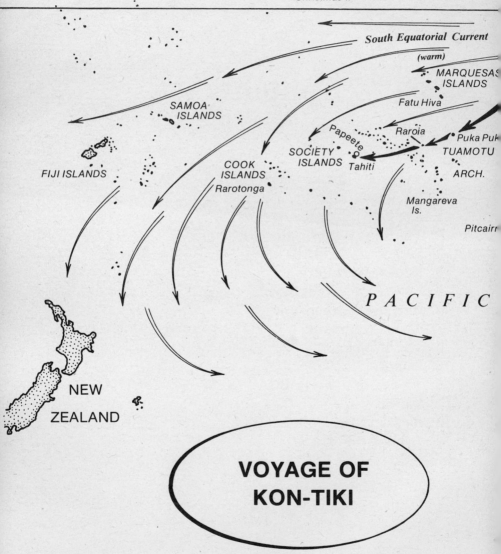

Christmas I.

South Equatorial Current

(warm)

MARQUESAS
ISLANDS

Fatu Hiva

SAMOA
ISLANDS

Papeete

Raroia

Puka Puk

TUAMOTU

SOCIETY
ISLANDS

Tahiti

ARCH.

FIJI ISLANDS

COOK
ISLANDS

Rarotonga

Mangareva
Is.

Pitcairn

PACIFIC

NEW

ZEALAND

VOYAGE OF
KON-TIKI

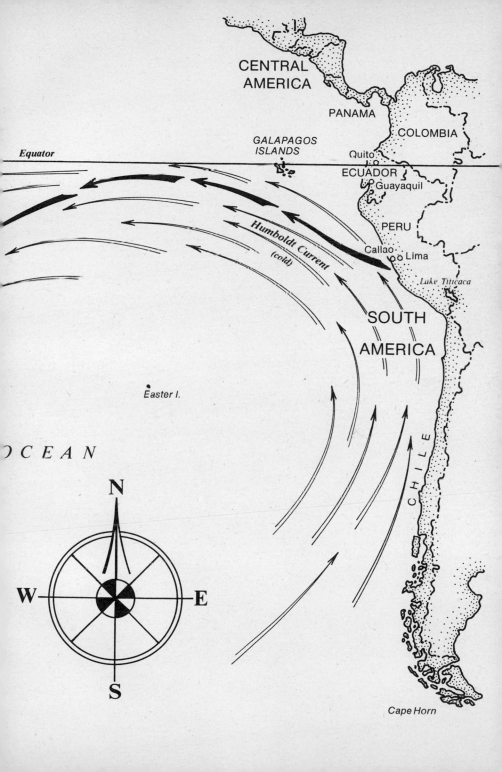

1.

Kon Tiki

THERE WERE SIX MEN and a green parrot on the raft.

Just ahead, pulling the raft, was a tug belonging to the Peruvian navy. Around both crafts circled a swarm of small boats, blowing horns and whistles. From the nearby piers people waved and cheered. The men on the raft looked at one another and grinned. "Well," one of them said, "at least we are getting a big send-off."

The parrot screamed in Spanish.

Slowly the tug moved past the harbor docks and into the open sea. Here the fleet of circling boats turned back. In the long, slow waves of the Pacific, the raft began to jerk and fight against its towline. A wave broke over the bow, rushing back around the feet of the six men before it drained away between the balsa logs.

"It's the towline that keeps the bow down," one of the men said. "*Kon Tiki* wasn't made to be towed. Tomorrow, when the tug turns us free, we'll do better." He added, "I hope."

The raft was forty-five feet long and about half that wide, made of logs of balsa wood. There was a small open cabin, roofed with split bamboo. In front of the cabin two masts leaned together to form an upside-down V. The sail was still rolled up at the bottom.

The entire raft was tied together with ropes. There was not a single piece of metal in its makeup. Many people believed the raft would fall apart with the first large wave that rocked it. Others claimed that after a few days in the sea, the logs of balsa would absorb water, grow heavy, and sink.

The six men on board were betting their lives that neither thing would happen. Ahead of them lay more than four thousand miles of empty ocean, from the coast of Peru to the Polynesian islands of the South Pacific. If completed, their voyage to these islands would be one of the most incredible in the recorded history of the sea.

All that first day and night the tug moved steadily westward. The raft followed, fighting against the towline like a bucking horse. Once the line broke and had to be repaired. The weather remained good, the Pacific as calm as it would ever be. But time and again waves broke over the raft's bow, and the men wondered what it would be like when they met a storm.

It was morning when the tug stopped. The raft now was fifty miles offshore and no longer a danger to steamships traveling along the coast of South America. The towline was cast off. The tug's whistle gave a long blast of good wishes and turned back east.

The raft was left alone.

The date was April 29, 1947.

The leader of the men on the raft was named Thor Heyerdahl. He was Norwegian, thirty-two years old, a lean, hard-muscled man with blond hair, blue eyes, and a nose like the beak of a hawk. The raft, its name *Kon Tiki,* and the incredible journey ahead were all his ideas. He had gathered together the five men with him, and now he felt responsible for their lives. As he watched the tug sail away, he knew there was a good chance that neither he nor any of the men with him would live to see another human being.

Even so, Thor Heyerdahl had spent many months and all his money fighting for the chance to be there, adrift on a raft of balsa. To him it was far more than simple adventure. He wanted to test a scientific theory: Heyerdahl believed that the first men to settle the Polynesian islands of the South Seas had come from the coast of South America. It was a theory at which most of the world's scientists merely laughed. Before Columbus reached South America, they said, the native Indians had no real ships and did not understand navigation. They had canoes and balsa rafts with which they could travel up and down the coast, dragging the rafts ashore now and then to dry out. But there was no possible way these craft could have crossed the Pacific.

Heyerdahl believed the early Polynesians had made the voyage on their balsa rafts. Across this vast stretch of ocean the trade winds blew steadily westward. The great Humboldt Current that flowed north along the coast of Chile swung to the west off the coast of Peru. A raft that followed the winds and current might make the journey— *if* it held together and did not sink.

Thor Heyerdahl thought of these things as he watched the tug disappear. A sudden feeling of loneliness had come over him and over the men with him. For a long while no one spoke. The raft rose and fell with the waves. Then one of the men joked, "Now we'll have to start the engine, boys."

That broke the spell, and they all laughed. "At least," Thor said, "we should put up the sail."

Not one of the six men was a professional sailor. In fact, only one of them knew much about the sea. Raising the sail, they worked awkwardly, getting in one another's way. But finally the sail was up. It was a square, orange-colored sail, and painted on it was the face of a man with a red beard and bulging eyes. This was Kon Tiki, the ancient Polynesian god.

The sail hung slack. It flapped with the swaying of the raft, but that was all. "Where's this prevailing wind that's supposed to blow us west?" said one of the men. It was meant as a joke, but now a nervous tension gripped them all. To Heyerdahl, staring down at the water, it seemed that not only the wind but the current also had failed. Instead of moving northwest, the raft was drifting back toward the coast of Peru.

The great experiment on which Thor had staked both his life and his reputation as a scientist seemed about to fail before it even began.

Then, suddenly, there was a noise like the crack of a gun. The sail billowed with wind. The masts creaked. And the *Kon Tiki* lurched into movement, northwest, as the trade wind began to blow.

Heyerdahl threw back his head and shouted, "Westward ho!" Now the other men were shouting too. The green parrot danced on the cabin roof and screamed in Spanish.

One of the strangest voyages in history had begun.

2.

The Boy
Who Could Not Swim

THOR HEYERDAHL had a lonely childhood. Both his father and mother had been married before, and both had children by their previous marriages. But Thor's half brothers and sisters were much older than he. They left home while he was still young, and Thor was raised as an only child.

His father was a well-to-do businessman in the town of Larvik, Norway. The Heyerdahl home was a large, comfortable house on a hilltop. Thor liked to stand in front of a window watching the ships come and go through Oslo Fjord. He wondered where they went and what strange lands lay beyond the horizon.

One winter day Thor went to watch blocks of ice being cut from a nearby lake. The ice was to be used in the brewery owned by Thor's father. Thor, happy to be out of doors, began to run excitedly about on the lake. He jumped onto a block of ice that had been cut free from the rest. Under the boy's weight it tilted slightly. Arms waving, Thor plunged into the icy water.

Fear and the shock of the cold water paralyzed him. He did not know how to swim. Fortunately, the air trapped inside his clothing kept him floating for a few moments. To the child, his mind black with terror, these moments seemed to last forever.

A workman reached him, caught the collar of his coat, and pulled him to safety.

The next summer Thor's father tried to teach him to swim. But even the thought of putting his face beneath the surface terrified Thor. "He'll learn as he gets older," his father said.

But Thor's fear of the water did not fade. Later his father hired a professional swimmer to teach the boy. Thor wanted to swim. He watched the teacher carefully. He learned exactly what he was supposed to do. But as soon as he stepped into the water, he would feel terror cold inside himself. And the instant his face went beneath the surface, blind panic took over.

This happened time and again. From his teacher

Thor learned everything there was to know about swimming—in theory. But in actual practice he simply could not swim. Finally his teacher told Mr. Heyerdahl, "This boy is never going to learn," and quit.

Though he was afraid of the water itself, Thor was fascinated by the beach, the shells, the life of the sea. He was still very young when he started a collection of seashells. As he grew older, his father introduced him to some of the commercial fishermen in Larvik. The boy spent hours around the fish houses, watching the boats being unloaded, asking questions. Fishermen brought him strange creatures that had been caught in the nets.

Thor's mother took him to the zoological museum in Oslo, the capital of Norway. He had never seen a museum before. He wandered wide-eyed from one exhibit to the next. When at last he was pulled away, he told his mother, "There's no museum in Larvik. So I'm going to start one."

Even at that age, if Thor set a goal for himself, he stuck to it. He talked his father into allowing him to use an old building near the brewery. The boy already had his collection of shells and the creatures of the sea, as well as butterflies and other insects. Now he began to collect all sorts of wildlife. Some of the other schoolchildren brought their collections. Before he finished high school, Thor had a real museum. It was so good that even the teachers in Larvik brought classes there to study.

It was not only the study of animals and insects that interested Thor, but all the outdoors. In winter he often went skiing with his father. In the summers his mother, a tall, athletic woman, took her son on long hikes through the mountains. Sometimes they camped outdoors for several days at a time. On one of these trips, miles from any town or even a road, they came upon a tumbledown log cabin. "What a strange place for a house," Thor said. "I wonder if anybody really lives here."

As he spoke, the door opened and a tall, bearded young man came out. His clothes were old, torn in places, but they had once been both expensive and stylish. "Good morning," he said, smiling. "I don't see many visitors back here in the mountains."

Thor's mother explained they were hiking and had had no idea there was a house anywhere near. The young man pointed to a bench beneath a tree where they might sit and rest. He brought them water to drink. While he and Mrs. Heyerdahl talked, Thor stared in wonder. To the boy this young hermit looked much like the Tarzan Thor had read about in books.

His name, the hermit told them, was Ola Björneby. His father had been a wealthy man who, a few years before, had lost all his money. Ola, well educated but with no specific training for a job, had decided to leave civilization and live alone in the mountains. Here, by farming and fishing in the summers and hunting in the winters, he earned his living. And in doing so he found a strange kind of contentment. He would never again go to live in a city.

When Thor and his mother left to continue their hike, they talked about the young hermit. He fascinated both of them. Later that summer Thor once more made the long walk into the mountains to visit Ola Björneby. Once when Ola went to Larvik for supplies, he visited Thor's home. And when Thor was fourteen, he was allowed to spend the entire summer with Ola.

It was a summer that Thor Heyerdahl would always remember. It was the first time he had ever had to do physical work: planting and hoeing a garden, cutting and carrying hay, repairing winter damage to the cabin. Thor could feel his muscles stretching and hardening under the summer sun. But it was not all work. He learned how to fish in the mountain streams. He learned to read the tracks of animals. He learned the feeling of independence.

Much of Thor's childhood had been lonely. Even in school, he had had few close friends. But here in the wilderness, there was no loneliness.

He felt at home among the trees, the towering mountains, the icy streams, as he had never felt in the crowded streets of Larvik or Oslo.

Years later, a world-famous man, Thor Heyerdahl would say that the summer he had spent with the hermit Ola Björneby had affected his whole life.

3.

Swim—or Drown!

By the time he was sixteen, Thor was determined that sometime, somehow, like Ola Björneby, he would leave civilization to live close to nature.

Just how he was going to do this, Thor did not know. But whenever there was a chance now, he went camping in the mountains. He did exercises, consciously strengthening his body against the unknown time when his life might depend on his physical strength.

At the university in Oslo Thor studied zoology. He was a good student, but he did not like living in the big city. He felt hemmed in by the buildings, the factories that polluted the sky with smoke and smell.

But it was in Oslo that Thor met Bjarne Kroepelien. Kroepelien had lived for years on the South Sea island of Tahiti, and he owned many books about these Polynesian islands and their people. Thor began to borrow the books and study them. He became convinced that somewhere in the South Pacific was the ideal island—a place where a man might truly return to nature.

It was about this time that Thor fell in love. The girl's name was Liv, and she was a very pretty girl with thick blond hair and blue eyes. Thor found he could talk to her about his dreams in a way he had never talked to anyone else.

"It seems to me," he told her, "that God created an earthly paradise. But man hasn't been satisfied with paradise; he wants progress. Imagine—progress in paradise!"

"It's a matter of economics," Liv said. She was studying economics at the university. "Civilization created money. Many people consider money the most important thing in life."

When Thor talked of his dream of going back to nature, Liv listened with interest. Thor showed her the books he had borrowed from Bjarne Kroepelien. They read them together. They spent hours poring over charts, learning all they could about individual islands. They would go to one together, they decided. But to which one? Some had too many tourists. Some were without fresh water or fruit trees that would make living there possible.

Finally they decided on what seemed the perfect island. Named Fatu Hiva, it was one in a group of islands called the Marquesas, about eight hundred miles northeast of Tahiti. According to the books, the climate was ideal. There were many fruit trees, streams of pure, fresh water, and few people.

Thor and Liv made their plans: they would be married as soon as Thor finished the university. Then they would head for Fatu Hiva to live.

But there was—as there usually is—a problem.

Once on Fatu Hiva they planned to live in such a way that money would be unnecessary. But first they had to get there, and that cost money. Thor knew his father would finance the trip, but only if he believed that what his son was doing was worthwhile. So Thor needed some reason for the trip besides getting away from civilization.

He talked to his professors. What kind of scientific work could a man and woman, living alone on a remote South Pacific island, carry on? "Well," one of them told him, "very little is known about the origin of the native animals and plants. How did they first get there and where did they come from? It would be an important contribution to science if someone could learn this."

Thor had studied zoology and botany. This was

the type of study he could make. Both his parents and Liv's agreed it would be worthwhile.

But neither Thor nor Liv told their families the full truth. Neither mentioned that if their experiment worked, they would not come back to Norway. They would spend the rest of their lives on Fatu Hiva, a sort of modern Adam and Eve in a South Pacific paradise.

On Christmas Day the newly married couple sailed from Oslo. Thor was just a few months past his twenty-second birthday. Liv was only twenty. Six weeks later they stood at the bow of the ocean liner watching the misty mountains of Tahiti rise slowly above the sea.

Fatu Hiva was still a long way off, but none of the big ocean liners went there. Now and then a small sailing ship left Tahiti to visit the Marquesas and buy coconuts. However, the next one did not plan to leave for several weeks. This gave the young couple time to visit a Tahitian chief named Teriieroo. Teriieroo was a close friend of Bjarne Kroepelien, the Norwegian who had lent Thor his books about the South Pacific.

From the Tahitian port where Thor and Liv had landed, it was a half day's trip by bus to Teriieroo's home. This was a small, tin-roofed cottage in a valley that ran from the mountains to a beautiful coral-ringed lagoon. Bananas and coconut palms grew all around, splashed with the bright red of hibiscus flowers.

Teriieroo was a huge, laughing, brown-skinned man with a fat but pretty wife. When Thor showed them the letter he had brought from Bjorne Kroepelien, Teriieroo welcomed them as if they were his own children. And when told they planned to live in the Marquesas, he insisted that first they stay with him to learn something practical about life in the islands. "You have read many books," he told Thor, "but do you really know when you see them, which plants you can eat and which are poisonous? Do you know how to climb a coconut palm or how to catch prawns in the streams? Does your bride know how to cook the red mountain banana, or how to bury breadfruit until it has fermented?"

In the weeks that followed, Thor and Liv learned these things and many more from Teriieroo and his wife. The Tahitians wore only *pareus,* brightly colored cloths wrapped around the body. So Thor and Liv dressed the same way. They learned to go barefoot, which was painful at first but very pleasant after the soles of their feet became toughened. Thor learned how to climb coconut palms like a monkey, with only his hands and feet touching the trunk and his body held clear.

Then came the day when Thor and Teriieroo went after prawns, shrimplike crustaceans found in both fresh and salt water. Thor decided to wade across to the other side of the river. He could see the bottom; the water was only about shoulder deep. But as he waded deeper, the old fear of drowning touched him. He moved carefully, sliding his feet forward a little at a time.

Something turned under his foot. He staggered, and the current knocked him off balance. Suddenly he was floundering, face under, being swept toward the open lagoon.

Panic exploded in his mind, a blind terror against which he could not reason. He felt his body turning, rolling with the water. He saw the bottom, the sky, then the bottom again.

And then, somehow, he got control of his mind. For an instant he forced himself to be still, to think. He knew what he was supposed to do to swim. A thousand times he had practiced the strokes on dry land. Now he began to use them in the water.

To his amazement he began to swim. He lifted his head and took a breath as he had been taught to do. He put his face back under the surface and kept swimming.

His hands touched the riverbank. He pulled himself out and stood up. For a few seconds he stood looking back at the river. Then he turned, half running, going upstream until he found a deep, still pool of water. Without pausing he dived in and began to swim, trying one stroke after another.

It was one of the great moments of Thor's life.

4.

Return to Nature

THOR AND LIV stayed with Teriieroo for a month. Then word came that a schooner was sailing for the Marquesas Islands. And so, at last, early one morning, Thor saw the blue-green mountains of Fatu Hiva rise out of the sea.

At first the island seemed to be one giant cliff topped with trees. Here and there small waterfalls plunged down the cliff into the sea. Then, as the ship moved slowly along the island, Thor saw a break in the cliffs. A valley led inland, incredibly beautiful with green trees and a river flowing down the middle. "This is where we must go ashore!" Liv cried.

The captain of the schooner shook his head. This valley, he said, was called Hanavave. At one time, far in the past, so many natives had lived here that it was divided into three kingdoms. Then the white men came, bringing unknown diseases. The Polynesians, who had no immunity and knew nothing of sanitation, died by the hundreds, then by the thousands. Now no more than fifty or a hundred persons were left in all Hanavave Valley. Many of these suffered from a disease called elephantiasis. The disease, caused by parasitic worms, was carried by mosquitoes, and it caused the victim's extremities to swell until they were almost as big as his body.

Hanavave was beautiful, but it was no place for two young Europeans to go ashore seeking paradise.

South of Hanavave there was another break in the cliffs, another beautiful green valley with a river flowing through it. This one was called Omoa. A few natives lived here, the schooner's captain told Thor. Some of them had elephantiasis, but not so many as at Hanavave. If Thor and Liv were determined to land on Fatu Hiva, this was the place.

A small boat was lowered over the side. Thor and Liv were rowed to a small, rocky beach and left. From where they stood there was no house visible, no road, no sign of life. Then, as they started to walk inland, they saw several brown-skinned men and women standing half hidden behind palm trees. Thor called to them, using a greeting he had learned from Teriieroo. The natives stared back at him without understanding.

An old woman shouted something Thor could not understand. So he spread his hands and laughed. Suddenly everyone laughed and ran forward. The old woman licked her finger and rubbed it across Liv's cheek. She looked at her finger and looked at Liv's cheek. Then she and everyone else laughed again.

It took the newcomers a moment to understand: white men had come to this island before, but never a white woman. The people had thought at first that Liv was a native girl who had been whitewashed.

There was one man in the Omoa Valley who could speak French, which both Thor and Liv knew. With his help they explored part of the valley. They were shown a place, far upstream from the native village, where a queen of Omoa had once lived. Here part of the mountainside had been leveled off. Terraces, almost like small pyramids, had been built by cutting blocks of stone and fitting them together. But now the terraces were wildly overgrown with jungle. Almost buried in this jungle were fruit trees of a dozen kinds. There was a beautiful spring of clear water in which prawns could be trapped. With the help of the natives, Thor and Liv cleared part of the jungle. They built a bamboo cottage and settled down to live.

For a while it was very much the paradise they had imagined. The stream and the fruit trees furnished plenty of food. The weather was perfect. Mosquitoes bothered them at night, but not too much.

Exploring the valley in which they lived, Thor and Liv collected dozens of beautiful, multicolored tree snails, along with beetles, butterflies, and many other insects. All these they preserved carefully for shipment back to the professors in Oslo. Neither of them thought of going back. Life in a tropical paradise was much too splendid.

In hunting for the insects and other creatures, Thor often found ancient stone tools. These had apparently been made by men long before the first Europeans had discovered these islands in the sixteenth century. Once he discovered a big stone statue of a fish. Near it he found the stone figures of short, fat men with bulging eyes. Along with these he found what seemed the strangest carving of all. It showed a crescent-shaped ship, curling sharply upward at bow and stern, and with a double mast. The only Polynesian ships that Thor had ever read about were canoes or rafts. Where had the man who carved this ship a thousand years or more before seen such a craft?

None of the people on Fatu Hiva could say. They merely whispered that all the statues were *tiki,* gods. *"Menui tiki!"* one told Thor, meaning, "Many gods."

More and more Thor began to wonder where these early Polynesians had come from. How had they learned to make terraces from smoothly cut blocks of stone? Why did all the stone statues of tikis have eyes so much alike? Vaguely he remembered having read a book by a German scientist who wrote that the pre-Columbian Indians of South America carved eyes like this.

Other things puzzled Thor. On the eastern side of the island the waves, driven by wind and current, broke in thundering masses. The trade winds always came from the east. And when Thor asked one of the oldest men on Fatu Hiva where his ancestors had come from, the native pointed east. He told of Tiki, a certain Tiki who was both god and man; it was this Tiki, he said, who had led the first people to Fatu Hiva. And they had come from the east.

But Thor knew that in Europe all the scholars said that the first Polynesians had come from the west, from Asia.

While Thor puzzled over these things, the

clouds blowing in on the trade winds grew darker day by day. Then the rainy season began. And the paradise that Thor and Liv believed they had found quickly changed.

As the rains poured down, the earth turned to a sea of mud. Vast numbers of insects moved into the bamboo cottage. Scorpions were bad, their stings cruelly painful. But the mosquitoes were even worse. Day and night they came in swarms. They got into Liv's eyes and nose. Their bites festered and turned into sores. And any one of the mosquitoes might, quite possibly, carry the parasitic worm that caused elephantiasis.

Both Thor and Liv developed sores on their arms, legs, and feet. The sores got larger. The rain kept falling, and the bamboo shelter became a soggy, moldy mess. Thor could scarcely walk because of the sores on his feet. Liv was sick, and there was no doctor on Fatu Hiva.

Finally, in a small boat along with a group of natives, they went to another island where there was medical help. Later, when the rains had stopped, they returned to Fatu Hiva, but it no longer seemed a paradise. When a schooner stopped to pick up copra, they took passage to Tahiti. There they boarded an ocean liner for Norway.

"At least we've learned one thing," Thor told Liv. "No one can buy a ticket to paradise. Happiness doesn't come from *where* one lives, but how."

"And now?" Liv asked.

He shook his head. He did not know that some ten years later he would be returning to these islands in a very strange and dangerous manner.

5.

"Balsa Logs Will Sink"

IN NORWAY THOR earned his living by writing articles and giving lectures about his experiences on Fatu Hiva. At the same time he kept reading, studying all he could about Polynesia. He still wanted to know where the island plants and animals had come from. But even more he wanted to know about the people themselves.

The old man of Fatu Hiva had told Thor that his ancestors had come from the east. A study of maps showed him that the great Humboldt (or Peru) Current flows northwest along the coast of Peru in South America, then west and finally southwest to the South Pacific islands. A boat following wind and current from Peru would eventually reach Polynesia.

But, the books told Thor, the South American Indians had no boats before the time of Columbus, only canoes or rafts that could not possibly cross an ocean.

Thor kept studying. He learned that, when the early Spanish explorers first reached South America, they found stone tools and carved gods much like those Thor had found on Fatu Hiva. And these early Spanish heard stories of an ancient god named Tiki—the word used for gods throughout Polynesia. Why would this name be the same if the people had never had contact?

After one of Thor's lectures, a man invited him to look at a collection of stone tools and human figures that he owned. To his amazement they were much like those he had seen on Fatu Hiva. More surprising, they had come neither from the islands nor from Peru. Instead they had been found on the west coast of Canada, in a remote valley called Bella Coola.

Could Indians from Canada have reached Polynesia as well as those from Peru? Thor wondered. A study of maps showed him that from Bella Coola the ocean current flowed west and south, toward the Hawaiian Islands. Thor decided to go to western Canada to carry on his studies.

By this time World War II had begun, but Norway was not yet involved. The war seemed far away and unimportant to Thor. He and Liv, with their new baby Thor Junior, sailed for Canada.

The Bella Coola Valley was a semiwilderness, where only a few people lived. Some of these were Indians. Thor began asking questions about their ancestors. He began digging at the sites of old villages. He found stone tools like those he had been shown in Norway—much like the ones he had seen on Fatu Hiva.

There was little time for research, however. In Europe Hitler's armies invaded Norway. The small Norwegian force was quickly defeated, but some units escaped to England to re-form. When Thor learned what was happening, he left Liv and Thor Junior with Canadian friends and went to New York. There an officer was enlisting men in the Norwegian air force.

Thor joined and was sent to Canada for training as a radio operator. Then he was sent to England for more training. Finally he was sent to Russia, and from there slipped secretly into a part of Norway that lay between the Russian and German battle lines. Thor's job was to keep the Allied headquarters in England in contact with the underground forces in occupied Norway. It was a lonely and dangerous job.

Thor was glad to do his best to help his country while the war lasted, but he was happy to be free

again. When the war ended, he at once returned
to his studies. Now he learned that when the
Spanish explorers first came to Peru, they found
the ruins of pyramids and of huge stone carvings,
some of them showing bearded men with bulging
eyes. These ruins were much like those Thor had
seen on Fatu Hiva. The Incas, Indians who were
ruling Peru when the Spaniards came, said that
the pyramids and statues had been made by a
race of tall, bearded men with light-colored skin
who ruled the country before their own time.
Their leader was named Kon Tiki, the son of the
sun. But there had been a war, and Kon Tiki and
his followers were defeated. They had fled to the
coast—and there they had vanished into the Pacific like the foam from a wave.

Many scholars of South American and Polynesian history had heard these stories. But they believed the stories to be mere legends, without
much truth. Thor, however, was now convinced
that the first people to reach Polynesia had come
from the coast of South America. He wrote a book
about it called *Polynesia and America, A Study in Prehistoric Relations.* In this he gave many of his reasons:
the trade winds and the currents that moved from
east to west; the name "Tiki" and other words
common to both the Indians of Peru and the natives of Polynesia; the building of stone terraces
in both places; the fact that Polynesians had long

skulls like those of the Indians, not round skulls
like the people of Asia. It was a long, very schol-
arly book.

When the manuscript was finished, Thor took
it to New York. There, on the top floor of a large
museum, he showed it to an old man, a great
scholar who had spent most of his life studying
Polynesian history.

The old man pushed the manuscript aside, re-
fusing to read it. "The pre-Columbian Indians
never crossed the Pacific Ocean for one simple
reason," the old man said. "They had no ships."

"But they had rafts of balsa wood," Thor ob-
jected. "Many of the Spanish explorers described
them. Some even drew detailed pictures. Such a
raft carried by current and wind would travel
steadily westward."

The old man shrugged. "Have you read the trea-
tise *Aboriginal Navigation off the West Coast of South
America,* by Dr. Lothrop of Harvard?"

"Yes, but—"

"Dr. Lothrop points out that balsa rafts were
used to travel up and down the coast. But the
balsa wood absorbs water. Unless pulled up on
the beach now and then to dry, it becomes heavy
and sinks. Such a raft could not possibly cross
the Pacific."

"Dr. Lothrop never actually tried a balsa raft,"
Thor said. "Maybe—"

But the great scholar was not listening. He pushed the manuscript toward Thor. "You can try a trip from Peru to the Pacific islands on a balsa raft if you wish," he said, and turned away.

Other scholars treated Thor's manuscript in much the same way. They said the pre-Columbian Indians could not have settled the Polynesian islands because they had no ships.

As Thor listened to one scholar after another, he remembered the old man in the museum saying, "You can try a trip from Peru to the Pacific islands on a balsa raft if you wish."

Finally he realized there was only one way to convince the scientific world that his theory was at least possible: he would have to make the trip from Peru to the Pacific islands on a balsa raft.

It was not the spirit of adventure that drove Thor Heyerdahl to a voyage most people believed to be not only impossible but suicidal. It was to prove a scientific theory. But along with his scientific turn of mind, Thor had inherited much of his father's business ability. In some ways he was as much a promoter as a scientist. Both sides of his nature were necessary to accomplish the amazing journey ahead.

To assemble a crew, fly to Peru, collect provisions for a three-to-four-month voyage, and to build the balsa raft would require a great deal of money. Thor had almost none. In fact, at this time he was so broke that he was living in the

Norwegian Sailors' Home in Brooklyn. This was not because he was a sailor, but because it was a place where Norwegians could live cheaply.

It was here that he met a tall, powerfully built young man named Herman Watzinger. Watzinger was no more a sailor than Thor; he was an engineer who specialized in refrigeration. When he heard of Thor's plan to cross the Pacific on a raft, he began to laugh. "It's crazy," he said. "But I'd like to go with you. Only I can't help with the money because I don't have any."

Thor's father would have helped. Since the war, however, Norwegian law prohibited the sending of money out of the country. Somehow Thor had to raise the money himself.

Thor worked at it in the same stubborn, single-minded manner with which he had followed his research. He persuaded the U.S. Air Force to furnish canned foods, waterproof sleeping bags, kitchen equipment, and other supplies they wanted tested for possible use by flyers downed at sea. He borrowed money, some from one source, some from another. He sent cablegrams to three old friends asking if they would join him. Two of these, Knut Haugland and Torstein Raaby, were Norwegian war heroes Thor had known when he was in the service. The other was a boyhood friend, Erik Hesselberg. All three wired back they would join Thor in Peru.

On his borrowed money Thor and Herman

Watzinger flew to Peru. There Thor got permission from the Peruvian government to build a balsa raft in the navy shipyard in Callao. At the same time he learned there were no balsa logs to be bought. The only way to get balsa logs of the size Thor needed was to go into the jungle. There he must cut down the trees, then float them downstream to Callao.

Thor asked the Peruvian air force to fly him and Herman into the jungle and drop them off by parachute, or to lend them a jeep and a driver who knew the country. He got the jeep and driver. And somehow the driver got the jeep over the mountains, across flooded rivers on rafts of balsa wood, and into the jungle where the big trees grew. There they cut the trees, bound them into a raft with rope, and floated them downstream to the sea.

(Though he did not know it at the time, the fact that dried logs of balsa were not available was a bit of wonderful luck. It would save the lives of Thor and his friends and make the voyage of the *Kon Tiki* possible.)

Thor had already spent weeks studying paintings and descriptions of balsa rafts left by early Spanish explorers. Now he worked to make sure the new raft was made exactly like those of the pre-Columbian Indians. First the nine largest logs were lashed together with ropes. Thor used no nails because the early Indians had none. Next, smaller logs of balsa were placed crosswise, one about every three feet, on the bigger ones, and lashed in place. On top of these smaller logs Thor and Herman placed a deck of split bamboo, lashed to the logs, with an open cabin of split bamboo and masts of mangrove wood.

Before the raft was finished, Thor and Herman Watzinger were joined by the three men who were to share the voyage. But Thor wanted still one more person for his crew. One morning a tall, red-bearded man knocked on Thor's hotel-room door and introduced himself as Bengt Danielsson. He was a Swedish scientist who had just finished an expedition up the Amazon River. In Peru he had seen newspaper stories about Thor's proposed voyage. "I'd like to go along," he said.

The two men became friends almost instantly. Later Thor wrote that any Swedish scientist who had the courage to go with five Norwegians on a raft was a man to cling to.

So it was that on April 28, 1947, six men with a green parrot for mascot left the harbor of Callao, Peru, on a raft. Because of the newspaper stories, crowds of people swarmed down to watch the departure. Many of them made bets on whether or not the men or raft would ever be seen again.

The odds were they would not.

6.

Into the Pacific

FOR A FULL HOUR after the tug had dropped its tow-line and the trade winds had begun to blow, the *Kon Tiki* moved slowly, steadily to the northwest. Waves came in long, slow rollers, and the raft moved easily up and down each one. The men on board began their individual duties.

The only member of the crew who actually knew much about the sea was Erik Hesselberg. Tall and sunburned, he looked like a professional sailor. Actually, he was an artist; it was he who had painted the face of *Kon Tiki* on the orange-colored sail. But he had also gone twice around the world on sailboats, and he knew navigation.

It was his job to "shoot" the stars and sun and plot the course of the *Kon Tiki.*

Herman Watzinger had some experience in aerology, and he was to serve as the amateur weatherman. Both Knut Haugland and Torstein Raaby were expert radio operators. They would broadcast weather reports to any ships or stations that might be listening. But the men all knew they would receive no reports about the seas they were to sail. The ocean ahead of them was not crossed by a single regular steamship or airline. A man— or a raft—lost in these waters would simply remain lost, forever.

Within two hours after the tug left them, the wind started to blow harder than before. By now the raft had moved into the mainstream of the Humboldt Current. Pushed by wind and current, the waves rose higher and higher. Since the *Kon Tiki* moved with the wind, the waves came at it from the stern. They seemed to rush at it, towering high over the heads of the men on board, threatening to crash down upon them. But each time the *Kon Tiki* rode smoothly up the slope of the wave and down the other side. When a wave did break over them, it was over the stern only. Then the water drained quickly away between the logs.

The big problem from the very first was steering. There was a huge, nineteen-foot-long steering bar fastened to the stern. But as the onrushing waves hit this, it was impossible even for two men to hold it steady. The tremendous force of the wave would knock the big oar to one side, almost hurling the steersmen into the sea. Also, when a wave did break over the stern, the steersmen got soaked.

Thor quickly realized that it was impossible to stop the raft, or turn it back against the wind and current. Once underway, there was no possibility of returning to the coast of Peru. Worse, if a man was washed overboard, there was no way to halt the raft until he was back on board.

So the first rule passed on the *Kon Tiki* was that the men at the steering oar must always be tied to the raft. Everyone took turns at the steering oar, two men at a time for two hours each.

There was little sleep the first night. A lantern swung on the mast overhead, the only light between the dark sea and the stars. The men at the steering oar watched the great waves rush at them from behind, loom overhead, then slide beneath them as the raft floated up the wave's breast. The men off duty lay close together in the small cabin trying to sleep.

The second night there was even less sleep. The wind had become a near gale, and the waves were onrushing monsters. They hurled the steering oar back and forth with such power the steersmen could not hold it at all. Working together, the whole crew managed to tie the oar with ropes.

Now the steersmen would hold the oar until just
before a huge wave struck. Then they would leap
forward to clutch lines fastened to the mast. There
they clung until the wave passed, then jumped
aft again to force the oar back into position.

With the next day the weather calmed a bit.
All the men had their sea legs now. Life on board
the *Kon Tiki* settled more or less into a routine.
When Erik Hesselberg took his sunsight and fig-
ured their position, he learned they were traveling
fifty-five to sixty miles a day northwest.

Thor looked at the position Erik had marked
on the chart. They were moving steadily toward
the Galápagos Islands, which lay across the equator ahead. In this area treacherous currents swept
in various directions.

"I wish we could steer *Kon Tiki* a little more
to the west," he said to Erik.

Erik shook his head. "We haven't learned much
about steering the raft yet. But both the Humboldt
Current and the trade winds should swing more
to the west before long."

The northward drift of the *Kon Tiki* was not
all Thor had to worry about now. He had noticed
that the balsa logs seemed to be getting soft. When
he pushed his finger against one, the wood gave
slightly, and water oozed out. He broke off a piece
of the water-soaked wood and dropped it overboard. The wood floated for a moment and then
sank.

Was it really true that logs of balsa would slowly absorb water until they became too heavy to float? This was what the old scholar in the museum had told him. But if so, how had men on balsa rafts made the voyage from Peru to the islands of the South Pacific? And Thor firmly believed that they had.

Later that day Thor saw Erik break off a small piece of log, drop it overboard, and watch it sink. Still later he saw Torstein Raaby do the same. None of the men knew he was being watched, and none of them said anything.

Day and night the *Kon Tiki* moved on. Gradually the current and the trade winds swung more to the west. In late May the *Kon Tiki* passed south of the Galápagos Islands, heading due westward now. But it rode lower in the sea than it had at first. There was no doubt the balsa logs were absorbing water.

Thor was also worried about the ropes that lashed the logs together. As the waves lifted one part of the *Kon Tiki* and dropped another, there was a constant stretching and straining. Lying on the bamboo floor of the cabin, Thor could hear the ropes rubbing against the logs. How long before this friction would wear the ropes thin? How long before they would break and the logs fall apart?

Early each morning one member of the crew would dive off the side of the raft, secured with a rope tether, and swim underneath. Looking up through the crystal-clear water, he would examine the ropes beneath the raft. And as days passed, it became obvious the ropes were holding, not wearing thin.

"I think I understand why," Thor said as he climbed back on the raft one morning. "The balsa logs are soft. As the ropes rub back and forth, they cut into the logs. As a result the ropes don't wear. And the logs are too thick to be cut apart."

The men on the raft lived so close to the sea that often they seemed to be a part of it. Almost every day some great school of fish swam close alongside. A man might lean over, select the fish he wanted for dinner, catch it by the tail and lift it on board. Flying fish skittered over the waves almost constantly. At night, if a lamp was left burning on deck, the flying fish were attracted to it. They flew into the side of the cabin or into the sail. Almost every morning there would be a half dozen or more on board. They were excellent eating. And one morning as Knut Haugland was cooking his breakfast, a flying fish zoomed on board and hit his hand. "Six inches to one side," Knut said, laughing, "and he'd have gone right into the frying pan."

Torstein Raaby did not laugh one night when he was awakened by the noise of something that hit the lamp, knocked it over, and put it out. There was no moon, and under the bamboo cabin it was pitch-dark. Then something cold and wet struck Torstein in the face. He thought it was a flying fish and clutched at it. It was long and scaly. It wrapped around his arm for a moment, slipped through his fingers, and fell on Herman, who was sleeping beside him. Within moments everybody in the cabin was floundering about, trying to get the lamp lighted and learn what had happened.

The visitor turned out to be a snakelike fish about a yard long, with huge eyes and razor-sharp teeth. Bengt Danielsson looked at it and shook his head. "You can't fool me," he said. "There's no such thing."

Bengt was almost right. Scientists later would identify the fish as *Gempylus,* a fish that during daylight hours lived at the bottom of the sea. A few skeletons had been found on the coast of South America, but the men aboard *Kon Tiki* were the first human beings ever to see one alive.

Thor knew the balsa logs had absorbed some water, but because of the constant rise and fall of waves, he could not tell if the raft was gradually sinking. One day when they had been at sea almost a month he took his knife and cut into a log. The first inch was water-soaked. The next inch was dryer, but still wet with water. The next inch showed only the natural sap of the log.

For a moment he could not understand. And

then he felt as if a great weight had been lifted from his shoulders. He knew now why some people said balsa logs would eventually grow heavy and sink. And he knew, too, that he had been extremely lucky that no dry balsa logs had been available when he built *Kon Tiki*.

Because Thor had cut fresh logs, filled with sap, and had plunged them immediately into water, their natural sap kept the seawater from soaking more than an inch or so into the logs. But if the logs had been sun-dried before going into the water, they would have lost their sap. Then the sea would have soaked deep into the logs until they were too heavy to float.

Thor felt certain now his raft would stay afloat. But he knew, too, that they were coming into a part of the Pacific where storms were more frequent than in the area they had already crossed.

7.

Man Overboard!

THE KON TIKI had been made with five center-boards. These were merely flat pieces of wood pushed down into the water between the bottom logs. On a boat with a rounded bottom these might have served as a keel to keep the vessel from turning over. But there was no danger that the flat-bottomed *Kon Tiki* might overturn. Thor had included the centerboards because he wanted his raft to be exactly like the one on which the god Kon Tiki and his followers had disappeared into the west. What, if anything, they were good for, he had no idea.

One morning Thor, carefully tied with a rope

as always, was swimming underneath the raft to examine the ropes. He saw that one of the centerboards had slipped loose. It took a lot of work to get it back in position. And while this was going on Erik Hesselberg, the navigator, made a discovery. The compass showed *Kon Tiki* was sailing almost due west. But as the centerboard was lifted higher in the water, the raft swerved a few degrees to the north. If the centerboard was pushed deeper into the water, *Kon Tiki* swung a few degrees south.

"So that's how the raftsmen must have navigated fifteen hundred years ago," Erik said. "When people quit using the rafts, the knowledge was lost."

Not long after this the first storm struck.

At first the trade wind slackened and died. The sky was a clear, still blue. Then off to the south a dark cloud seemed to rise out of the sea. Swiftly it grew bigger, turning from dark blue to black. A sudden wind sprang up from the south. With equal suddenness it stopped, then blew hard from the north. The *Kon Tiki* turned, sail flapping wildly.

The storm struck with a howl, blowing sheets of rain into the faces of the men. Together they fought to get the sail down and lashed to the bamboo boom before it blew away. Waves fifteen feet high and more crashed on the *Kon Tiki*'s stern, washing waist-deep around the steersmen.

At first Thor and every man aboard watched

the great waves with dismay. In such a sea, a round-bottomed vessel much larger than *Kon Tiki* might have overturned. But the raft rode up each wave, then down the other side. When a wave did crash on the stern, it quickly drained away between the logs.

For twenty-four hours the storm blew, then died away. Later someone noticed that the green parrot was missing. No one had seen it go. Probably a wave, breaking across the deck, had washed it overboard.

Every man on board felt the loss of the parrot. But there was no way to go back and look for it. With the centerboards they now could change the *Kon Tiki*'s course by a few degrees. But there was no way to stop the raft or to turn back. It was something each man understood but did not talk about.

At the beginning of July, following the curve of trade wind and current, the *Kon Tiki* was moving southwest. Squalls came every few days. During each one Herman Watzinger would duck in and out of the bamboo cabin with his anemometer to measure the force of the wind.

It was during one of the squalls that a gust of wind caught Torstein's empty sleeping bag and blew it across the deck. Herman, standing just outside the cabin with his anemometer, saw the bag blow past him. He jumped to catch it, slipped, and went over the side. When he came to the surface, the *Kon Tiki,* blowing before a fifty-mile-an-hour gale, was already out of reach.

Both Thor and Torstein saw Herman fall. "Man overboard!" they screamed. Torstein grabbed the coiled line attached to the rubber life raft. If he could get the life raft overboard with two or three men in it, they might be able to reach Herman, then be pulled back to the *Kon Tiki.*

For the first and only time on the voyage, the line tangled and refused to come loose. Together Torstein and Thor struggled to get it free.

Knut and Erik had grabbed life rings and hurled them toward Herman. But Herman was behind the *Kon Tiki* now. The life rings had to be thrown into the teeth of the wind, and the howling wind blew them back on deck. Knut and Erik threw them again, and again they blew back.

Herman was a strong swimmer, and now, following the *Kon Tiki,* he swam as he had never done. But it was impossible to keep up. Every moment the distance between him and the raft increased.

Knut Haugland caught the life ring blown back by the wind. This time he did not throw it. Instead, with one arm through the ring, he dived overboard. Bobbing up and down, kicking, swimming with his free arm, he fought his way toward Herman. Herman, swimming with every ounce of his strength, helped close the gap.

The two men reached one another. Both held to the life ring. Slowly, desperately, the men on board *Kon Tiki* hauled them back to the raft.

8.

The Wreck

For a long while the men on the *Kon Tiki* had seen no birds except now and then a small petrel. These were birds that made their home on the open sea and needed no land base for rest and sleep. Then on July 3 the men saw frigate birds far to the west.

"Frigates can go a thousand miles to sea and back," Thor said. "But seeing them means we're much closer to the islands than we were."

Erik pointed to the chart on which he had just marked the *Kon Tiki*'s location. "We are almost due east of your old island, Fatu Hiva."

"Maybe we'll make landfall there," Thor said.

Then he remembered the tremendous waves he had seen crashing against the windward side of the island, and added, "If so, I hope it's on the west side, where the seas are calmer."

But the wind and current were steadily carrying them southwest. Thor soon knew they would pass to the south of Fatu Hiva.

At dawn on July 30, Herman climbed the swaying mast to look around. A few seconds later he was on deck, shaking Thor out of his sleep. "An island!" he shouted.

It was the ninety-third day at sea. The island was Puka Puka, and it lay to the northwest. And no matter how they tried to steer *Kon Tiki* to the north, they passed south of the island.

Three days later another island became visible. This time it lay almost dead ahead. But as they came closer, they could see it was fringed by a coral reef. Against the reef the Pacific rollers built into gigantic waves. To try to cross the reef would mean a certain wreck. So once more the *Kon Tiki* sailed past an island, still going west.

Next day, working over his chart, Erik's face became very serious. He called Thor. "We are right here," he said, pointing to a spot about five hundred miles northeast of Tahiti. "And right ahead of us"—he moved his finger—"are the Raroia and Takume reefs. About fifty miles of unbroken reef. Unless we can steer much more to the south than we have been doing, we're going to wreck."

The sail was set, the centerboards set, the steering oar pushed as far over as it would go. But now they were in an area where the islands themselves caused varying currents. A small northwest current caught *Kon Tiki.* Slowly, steadily, the raft was driven toward the great reef.

Thor called his crew together. They had crossed the Pacific Ocean on a balsa raft. They had proved it could be done. But now at the very end came the most dangerous part—the time when they might all be killed together.

Quietly they talked over what should be done. Each man had his own ideas, but it was Thor who had to make the final decisions. Quietly he gave his orders.

The cameras, the radio equipment, everything that might be damaged by water was put into waterproof bags. Everything on the *Kon Tiki* was tied down even more securely than it had been. Over the radio Torstein sent messages giving their location and telling what lay ahead. He could not be sure that anyone heard.

By the time everything was ready, they could see the tops of palm trees dead ahead. These were on a small island ringed by a curving white beach. Outside the beach was a lagoon, as blue and still as the sky overhead.

But between the lagoon and the *Kon Tiki* was the reef.

At first it did not look dangerous. From the low

deck of the *Kon Tiki* they could see waves building up against the reef, but could not see them breaking over it. They could hear the sound, though— a rolling, dull thunder that grew steadily louder.

Once more Thor repeated the most important of all his orders: every man was to stay on the *Kon Tiki* at all costs. After the raft struck the reef, the waves would, eventually, lift and carry it across to the lagoon. But a man overboard would be battered to death against the sharp coral. Each man was to choose his own position, something he could hold on to, and stay with it.

The *Kon Tiki* was moving faster now, rising with the great waves that built higher and higher as they rushed toward the reef. And now they could see where the waves, one after another, struck the reef, mounted skyward, and came crashing down like some gigantic Niagara.

Thor's position was near the stern, clinging to a rope tied securely at both ends. Looking back he saw a wave bigger than any he had ever seen. It blotted out the sky for a long, breathless moment—and came down.

He thought he was being crushed by the weight of the water. Then the weight was gone, but the water tore at him with incredible force. Arms and legs wrapped around the line, he hung on.

Suddenly the water was gone. Thor could breathe. He lifted his head and saw the rest of his crew all clinging to their positions. Then a second wave smashed down on *Kon Tiki*, bigger than the first.

Once more Thor thought he was being torn free of the line to which he held. It seemed to him his arms would be pulled from their sockets, his clenched fingers torn from his hands. But once more the wave passed. Once more, there was a brief instant in which he could see that the raft still held together, and his crew was still on board.

Then came the next wave, the biggest of all, and *Kon Tiki* smashed into the reef. After that Thor could not be certain of anything except the unbelievable weight and force of the water. His arms and legs were still wrapped around the rope, but he was moving—where, how, he did not know. He could not see or breathe, and his lungs were bursting.

Then the wave pulled back. Air rushed into his lungs. He opened his eyes and saw that the *Kon Tiki* was smashed. The masts were down. The cabin was flat. Logs pointed in various directions like a pile of jackstraws. Only one man was visible, and he lay flat, motionless, arms spread.

His great experiment had gone horribly wrong, Thor thought. What good was it to prove that men could cross the Pacific on a balsa raft if it cost the lives of his friends?

Then the man stretched flat on the deck moved,

looked around, and grinned. From under the wreck of the cabin came two others.

Another wave struck and sucked back again. But the *Kon Tiki* had been lifted well onto the reef now. By moving to the forward end of the raft the men could avoid most of the force of the waves. And all of the men were still alive, still uninjured. The water in the lagoon beyond the reef was no more than waist deep. Across this the men began to wade, carrying provisions from the wrecked *Kon Tiki* to the island.

The island itself was uninhabited and unnamed. But once the radio was ashore and had dried out, they made contact with French authorities on another island. They gave their geographic location and told what had happened. The date was August 7.

Soon afterward the radio began to crackle with a new message: a ship was on its way to rescue them *and* the *Kon Tiki*.

9.

Fame

BACK IN THE UNITED STATES, Thor found that he was suddenly famous. Newspapers had picked up and reprinted radio messages from the *Kon Tiki* as it crossed the Pacific. President Truman invited Thor and his crew to the White House. It was a wonderful thing, Truman said, to have people in the world who could take hardships and do a job such as these men had done.

But Thor had not made his voyage for fame. It had been to prove a scientific theory. Yet, to his amazement, many of the world's most famous anthropologists still laughed at his idea of westward migration across the Pacific. His voyage had been a childish adventure, a publicity stunt, these men said. It had proved nothing scientifically.

Thor was deeply hurt by the rejection of his theory by so many famous scientists. But other things required his immediate attention. All the money he had borrowed had to be paid back.

To do this Thor returned to Norway and gave lectures about his journey. Later he went on tours through Sweden, the United States, and England. Due to his constant traveling, he and Liv saw little of one another. Eventually they were quietly divorced.

Thor's lectures were well received, but they made little money. And at first a book about his experience, called *Kon Tiki*, seemed to be a failure. Then suddenly it became a best-seller. Translated into more than sixty languages, it was read avidly all over the world. At the same time, the *Kon Tiki* itself, now in Norway, was turned into a museum, drawing big crowds. Pictures taken on the Pacific voyage were made into a movie. And Thor was not only able to pay off his debts, he became moderately rich.

As Thor's popular fame spread, the scientific world became more and more split over what the voyage of the *Kon Tiki* really meant. Certainly it had proved that a balsa raft could cross the Pacific. But did that prove that the Polynesian islands had been settled from the west?

Thor himself had never claimed that the *Kon Tiki*'s journey alone would prove this. But it was, he said, proof that it *might* have happened that way. The real proof, he said, lay in other things: the similarity of the people of Polynesia and Peru and of their languages; the many plants and animals that were the same in both areas; the tools and crafts that were alike; the story of Kon Tiki himself. Thor had listed many of these things in his manuscript *Polynesia and America, A Study of Prehistoric Relations.* But that manuscript had never been published. Very few of the world's scientists had ever seen or heard of it.

Now that his debts were paid, Thor went back to the thing he really wanted to do. Once more he began to study everything he could find about both the pre-Columbian Indians of South America and the early Polynesians. He began to rewrite and add to his manuscript of *Polynesia and America.* This time he had no trouble finding a publisher.

In 1952 the book, now called *American Indians in the Pacific,* appeared in Sweden, England, and the United States. One famous scientist who reviewed it wrote:

Anyone who opens this volume of 821 pages cannot fail to be dazzled by the overwhelming knowledge which he displays. If Thor Heyerdahl had not prepared us in ad-

vance for the feat, one would have asked
oneself how it could have been possible
for a single man to read so many works
in so few years, make extracts from them,
and present the result of the investigations
in a true collection of facts from the sciences
of ethnology, archaeology, linguistics, botany, geography, and history.

Thor's book did not convince everyone that he
was right. But from this time on Thor was gener-
ally recognized not only as a man of adventure,
but as a true scientist.

Even while the arguments over his work continued, Thor went on with his studies. With two
other scientists he visited the Galápagos Islands,
which lay across the equator a few hundred miles
west of South America. Here they found the first
proof that prehistoric Indians had visited the area.
He remarried and with his new wife went to Lake
Titicaca in Peru to study the ruins of an ancient
and unknown civilization.

Half-buried in a tropical forest Thor found the
ruins of an ancient city in which thousands of
people had once lived. Among the ruins there were
great pyramids much like those of Egypt. There
were also terraces, stone tools, and many carved
figures of gods and fish and crescent-shaped boats
strangely like those Thor had seen on Fatu Hiva.

In fact, on Lake Titicaca the Indians still used crescent-shaped boats made of reeds. These looked
not only like the stone figure Thor had found on
Fatu Hiva, but almost exactly like pictures painted
on the walls of ancient Egyptian pyramids.

How had knowledge of such boats spread from
one side of the world to the other?

Thor knew that the Indians who greeted Columbus had told stories of light-skinned, bearded men
who had lived here untold years before. But, like
tales of Kon Tiki, most scholars considered these
mere legends and nothing more.

Continuing his studies, in 1955 Thor led a scientific expedition to Easter Island. Located more than
two thousand miles west of South America, Easter
Island is one of the most remote spots in the world.
The first Europeans to discover it, in 1722, were
amazed to find giant statues of heads carved from
solid rock. But when they asked the people of
Easter Island who had made the statues and why,
no one knew. They had been made a long, long
time ago.

There were many caves on the island, and in
some of these Thor found pictures of reed boats.

Next, Thor went to Egypt to study. In the muse-
ums and in some of the pyramids he found not
only pictures of reed boats but exact descriptions
of how they had been made.

For several years Thor went on with his studies

in Egypt, Europe, and America. All the while his mind kept going back to the *Kon Tiki* riding the west-flowing winds and current from Peru to the Polynesian islands. He knew that from the coast of North Africa the Equatorial Current flowed southwest and west toward America. The wind blew westward too. Perhaps men had followed wind and current across the Atlantic long before Columbus. Perhaps the descendants of these men had sailed on into the Pacific. Perhaps . . .

Thor Heyerdahl decided to build a crescent-shaped boat of reeds exactly like those of the ancient Egyptians. Then he would see if such a boat could sail from Africa to America.

10.

To Sea
in a Paper Boat

WHEN THOR HEYERDAHL built the *Kon Tiki,* he had wanted to prove that the first Polynesians might have come from America. Now he wondered if the South American Indian legend about bearded men who came from the east in the dawn of time could be based on fact also.

"This time I'm not trying to prove anything," Thor told a friend. "According to the best scientific knowledge, the Egyptians had quit building their pyramids and reed boats centuries before those of Peru were begun." He smiled. "It's all a riddle, and I don't claim to know the answer. But I want to take one step toward learning. I want to find out if a boat of reeds like those of the Egyptians can cross the Atlantic."

Thor quickly learned that building such a boat would require even more time, work, and money than building the *Kon Tiki*. The papyrus reeds no longer grew in Egypt in large numbers. But they did grow around some of the lakes deep in the heart of Africa, and Thor went there.

He found the natives sailing small boats of reeds, but the boat Thor wanted had to be forty-five feet long. It would require literally hundreds of thousands of reeds. He had to hire men to cut them. He had to find ways to have them hauled from one country to another, across vast areas without roads or railroads. Finally they arrived in huge piles at the foot of an Egyptian pyramid where the building was to take place.

The shipbuilders were two men Thor had brought from the heart of Africa. They had built many boats on their lake, but never one near the size Thor wanted. For a model they had only pictures. And though Thor spoke English, French, and Italian as well as his native Norwegian, everything had to be done through Abdullah, an African interpreter, for the shipbuilders spoke only Arabic.

Back in Peru many experts had told Thor that balsa logs placed in water would soon sink. Now Egyptian experts told him the same thing about papyrus reeds. To prove this, the director of a museum put a cut reed in a pan of water. Two weeks later it lay waterlogged on the bottom. Also, Thor knew that on some lakes the natives often hauled their boats onto land to dry. But on other lakes, boats were left in the water. Thor believed the reeds absorbed water through the cut ends. If these ends were tightly tied, as they must be in a large boat, it would keep the water from entering. At least, he hoped so.

There were other experts who said it did not matter whether the reeds sank or not, because in any case they would soon fall apart. They pointed out that the papyrus reed was the material from which ancient Egyptians made paper. They called Thor's craft a paper boat. They said it was suicide for men to try to sail it across an ocean.

Then there was the matter of fire. The papyrus reeds burned like paper. One match could send the ship up in flames.

Thor called his ship the *Ra.* In both Egypt and Peru, Ra had been the name of the ancient sun god.

While the *Ra* slowly took shape at the foot of an Egyptian pyramid, Thor was busy assembling his crew. On the *Kon Tiki,* there had been five Norwegians and a Swede. This time Thor wanted a small United Nations. This would symbolize the joining of the Old World and the New, as an earlier *Ra* might have done some thousand years or more in the past.

Abdullah, the African interpreter, agreed to

come along. He was an excellent carpenter, but he knew nothing about sailing and had never even seen an ocean.

The *Ra*'s doctor was a Russian, Yuri Senkevich. He had just spent a year with a scientific expedition near the South Pole, but he knew nothing about sailing.

The photographer was Carlo Mauri, an Italian. Red-bearded and blue eyes, he was a mountain climber as well as photographer, but he was not a sailor.

To represent Egypt, there was Georges Sourial, a professional diver. He told Thor, "I know the sea much better from underneath than from above." He laughed and added, "Judging by the looks of this boat, we may be underneath the water more than above it before the voyage is over."

Dr. Santiago Genoves was a Mexican anthropologist. He knew as much about the vanished civilizations of Peru and Mexico as did Thor. But he knew nothing about sailing ships or the sea.

The only real sailor in the lot was Norman Baker, from the United States.

Every member of the crew spoke more than one language. On the other hand, no one language was understood by all. Orders would have to be given in French, English, and Italian before every member of the crew would understand.

Thor had hoped to sail in early May. He wanted to cross the Atlantic before the hurricanes of late summer and autumn began to howl. But one problem came up after another. Finally, however, the *Ra* was finished.

It was a strange-looking vessel with its sharply curved bow and stern. It looked even stranger, standing where it had been built, in the middle of a desert at the foot of a pyramid.

Thor had chosen this building place deliberately to dramatize the connection between his planned voyage and the civilization of ancient Egypt. Now the *Ra* was placed on a sled much like those used to transport the great building blocks of the pyramids. Five hundred Egyptian athletes pulled it across the desert to the nearest paved road. Here it was put on a modern truck and taken to the Moroccan seaport Safi. Safi is on the northwest coast of Africa, facing the Atlantic, almost due east of Cape Hatteras.

In Safi all the members of the crew met for the first time. And on May 25, 1969, they were towed out of the harbor by four rowboats. On the Atlantic, the rowboats cast off their lines and turned back. The *Ra* sailed on. It would need good speed to reach the Americas before the hurricane season.

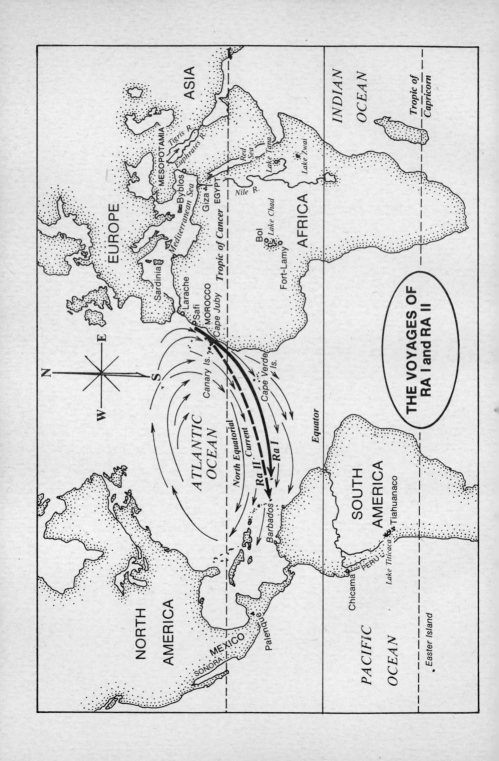

THE VOYAGES OF RA I and RA II

11.

Storm!

THE VOYAGE did not start well.

Norman Baker, the only real sailor on board, was sick with the flu. By the time the rowboats had turned back and Baker had helped get the sail up, he was too sick to walk. Yuri, the Russian doctor, put him to bed in the small cabin.

The wind, which should have been blowing out of the northeast, blew from the northwest. Despite the crew's desperate efforts, the *Ra* headed more south than west. Not far to the south of them the coast of Africa bulged westward, and a southerly course would smash *Ra* ashore.

The wind increased, still from the northwest.

The *Ra* had two long steering oars at the stern, and Thor and Georges Sourial pushed them as far over as possible, trying to turn the ship westward. The wind built to a near gale.

With a noise like two rifle shots, both oars broke.

While Thor and the others stood helpless, expecting the *Ra* to swing in toward the coast, it turned, very slightly, in the other direction. For a moment no one could understand. Then Thor began to laugh, remembering how the centerboards on the *Kon Tiki* had acted as rudders. The *Ra* had been built with two rowing oars, as well as steering oars, one on each side. Not being used, they were tied pointing straight down into the water. Now they, too, were acting as rudders.

Even so, it was impossible to turn due west. Instead, *Ra* moved southward, much too near the coast for comfort.

The wind began to swing from one direction to another in sudden squalls. Time and again the inexperienced crew fought to raise or lower the sail. Then on the morning of the second day, a sudden gust snapped the wooden yardarm that held the sail outspread. The sail began to flap wildly, threatening to rip apart. Somehow the crew got it down and furled.

Without either sail or rudder, there was no way to steer at all. And at this point the North Equatorial Current moved almost straight down the coast. The *Ra* moved with it, riding the great waves like a cork. The African coast lay only a few miles to the east.

On the third day the storm blew itself out. Abdullah, the carpenter, repaired one steering oar and the yardarm. The sail was raised again. The crew was learning to work together now, and the sharply curved bow of the paper boat swung more to the west.

Abdullah was a Muslim. Several times each day he washed himself in seawater, then faced west to pray. On this third day he dipped up a bucket of seawater to bathe and gave a startled cry. The water in the bucket was filled with black lumps and blobs.

"Oil," Thor said grimly. "A ship must have pumped its bilges."

There was no ship in sight. But as far as they could see around them, the blue-green ocean was made scummy with blobs of oil. The oil lasted all day. From this time on they saw it almost every day, often mixed with drifting beer cans and garbage.

It took a full week for the *Ra* to clear the westernmost bulge of Africa. By now the weather was better. Norman Baker was well again, and the men had learned to work together like professional sailors. Each day the *Ra*'s curving bow pointed into

the setting sun. With wind and current they were
averaging about sixty miles a day.

Again the weather changed. One squall followed another, with brief intervals between. The
Ra rode through them easily. But on the windward
side, where waves frequently splashed over the
rail, the papyrus was beginning to absorb more
and more water. The *Ra* began to tilt slightly into
the wind.

Whenever the sea calmed somewhat, Georges
would dive down and swim underneath the craft
to check the ropes that held it together. Georges
always had a line tied around his waist when he
swam. *Ra* handled better than *Kon Tiki;* even so
it could not be stopped or turned about to save
a man overboard.

They had been at sea about a month when
Georges came up from one of his dives frowning.
The whole stern of *Ra,* he said, was sagging.

Thor tied a line around his waist and dived
down to see for himself. Sure enough, the *Ra's*
bottom no longer ran in a straight line from the
curve of the bow to the curve of the stern. Instead,
the whole bottom aft of the cabin was sagging.

A few days later it was not necessary to swim
under the vessel to see that the stern was sinking.
The tail of the ship still curled forward, high above
the water. But between it and the cabin *Ra* rode

so low that even small waves sloshed over the rail.

Thor got out his detailed drawings of the ancient Egyptian ships. *Ra* had been built exactly like these—except for one thing. On the drawings a rope ran from the tip of the curled stern down to a beam behind the cabin. When the *Ra* was being built, Thor had believed this line was intended to keep the curved stern from straightening out. His African shipbuilders had insisted it was not necessary. The papyrus reeds, once bent into shape and dried, they said, would never straighten. On the small lake boats these men had built, there was no such rope from curved stern to deck. And so it had been omitted from *Ra.*

Thor called Norman Baker to study the drawings with him. "I think I understand now," he said at last. "This rope was not to keep the tail from straightening. It was to keep the back part of the boat from sagging."

"And I'm afraid it's too late to do much about it now," Norman said.

It was. Ropes were run under the sagging bottom. The whole thing was pulled up as much as possible and made fast. But aft of the cabin, the *Ra* continued to sink, little by little. Forward, the *Ra* rode clear and easily over the waves. But behind the cabin, waves broke steadily across the deck.

The weather got worse. The sagging stern acted like a sea anchor and slowed the ship's speed. Also, it made steering difficult and sometimes impossible. They had been at sea about five weeks when Norman told Thor, "If we were traveling in a straight line, we'd be in the West Indies by now. But we keep swinging, first north, then south."

Even so, they were less than a thousand miles from South America. Despite one storm after another, despite her sagging stern, *Ra's* bow rode high. Her sail billowing in the wind, the paper craft moved steadily westward. Over the radio Thor heard that a small ship carrying a moving-picture cameraman was coming to meet them. It should arrive in a few days.

The weather continued to be bad. Squalls followed one another. Then late in the afternoon of July 12, the sky to the south turned blue-black. Lightning split the blackness. Like some gigantic wall crashing down from the sky, a great storm swept across the sea and struck them.

Thor could never remember in detail the three days that followed. Wind and waves drowned out the sound of thunder. It was impossible to stand on deck without clinging to the mast or to lines from it to the cabin. No one moved without a rope around his waist, the other end made fast. Wind lashed the wave tops, the salt water min-

gling with the rain driven in level sheets. One
wave after another crashed over the deck. They
smashed the cabin walls and roof into a soggy
mess.

Dr. Santiago Genoves unfastened the rope
around his waist, meaning to tie it in another place.
At that instant a wave struck, lifted and hurled
him outward. By sheer luck his hand caught a
corner of the torn sail. He held on until the wave
passed, and Thor hauled him back to safety.

On July 16 the storm blew itself out. The *Ra*
still floated. At least, part of it did. Except for
its high, curled tail, the entire stern half was under
water.

Over the radio came word that the ship carrying
the motion-picture cameraman was searching for
them. They were asked to send up rockets to help
the ship locate them.

From beneath the wreck of the cabin Thor dug
up the box of rockets. It was marked "Keep in a
Dry Place." Looking at it, Thor and the others
began to laugh. The rockets were a soggy mass,
impossible to use.

Even so, keeping in contact by radio, *Ra* and
the cameraman's ship finally found one another.
One look at the condition of *Ra*, and the other
ship's captain was anxious for the crew to abandon
their paper boat and come on board. But Thor's
crew refused. They were within a few hundred

miles now of the island of Barbados. One after another, the crew told Thor, "We set out to make it all the way across. Let's keep on."

They did for another two days, the cameraman's motorship staying close. But now the radio weather reports told of a great hurricane forming to the east and moving toward them. Thor made the sad decision to abandon ship. "No scientific experiment is worth a man's life," he said. "Anyway, I set out to learn if a papyrus ship could cross the Atlantic. I know now that it can." He gave the orders. The important papers and film on board *Ra* were ferried by rubber raft to the motor ship. The *Ra*'s crew followed. The paper ship, her curled bow still high in the air, was set adrift.

12.

Ra II
and the Polluted Sea

THOR WAS NEVER QUITE SURE why he decided to build a second reed ship and set out once more to cross the Atlantic.

Partially, it was the urging of his crew. Every one of them wanted to try the voyage again. They wanted to prove that now, with more experience, they could make it all the way. Thor did also.

But there was another reason. After his first voyage, Thor had reported to the United Nations and told officials about the pollution he had found on the Atlantic. These people were amazed. Looked at from an airplane or the high deck of an ocean liner, such pollution was barely noticeable. Was it true that man was destroying the oceans, the source of all life?

Thor knew that many, perhaps most people thought of the oceans as being so vast they could not be harmed. But Thor, who had lived so close to both the Atlantic and Pacific, knew better. He knew that much of the seas' blue-green color came from plankton—tiny, almost microscopic bits of animal and plant life. It was incredibly numerous, but also fragile. It could be destroyed by a floating film of oil, or by industrial wastes pumped into the oceans by the sewers of the world. And it was this fragile, drifting plankton that created most of the molecules of oxygen that made all animal life possible, both in the sea and on land. If man destroys the oceans, he will also destroy himself.

Thor himself had not paid much attention to the great oil spills when he first saw them. Only gradually had he realized how vast the pollution was. A second trip on the low deck of a paper boat would give him a better chance to study it.

And so, not long after *Ra I* was left drifting off the coast of Barbados, Thor was busy with the construction of *Ra II.* This time the vessel was built in Safi, Morocco, the African port from which *Ra I* had sailed. And this time the shipbuilders were Indians from South America. The reed boats that sailed Lake Titicaca were larger than those on the lakes of Central Africa, their builders more skilled with big craft. They knew the secret of keeping the stern of a reed boat from sagging.

So it was that, in the spring of 1970, slightly less than one year after *Ra I* had put to sea, *Ra II* sailed from the same port. The crew was the same, except for Abdullah, who had to return home. He was replaced by another African, Madani Ait Ouhanni. Also, there was an extra cameraman along, a Japanese named Kei Ohara. It was truly a United Nations crew.

The steering oars on *Ra I* had broken the first day. From that time on its course had been determined more by wind and current than by human effort. *Ra II* was more skillfully built, her crew more experienced. They skimmed down the coast of Africa at eighty, ninety, even a hundred miles a day. Where the coast of Africa bulged westward, the current, the wind, and *Ra II* swung westward also.

There were storms. There were long days when giant waves threatened to swamp the tiny craft. But always the paper boat rode safely over them. For a while the voyage went so smoothly it was almost boring.

Day after day they passed floating streaks and blobs and lumps of oil. Sometimes the oil lumps were no bigger than a pea; sometimes they were as big as a man's fist. They clung to and fouled the reed sides of *Ra II*. Sometimes the oil covered miles upon miles of the ocean's surface, so thick Thor could not even find clean water in which to dip his toothbrush. Along with the oil, there was often a clutter of beer cans, bottles, and the garbage dumped from ships.

"I spent a hundred and one days on *Kon Tiki,*" Thor told the others. "My nose was as close to the water then as it is now. But we saw nothing like this. Look." They were passing through a vast area smeared with blobs of oil. Among these swam a few jellyfish, looking like blue-and-purple balloons floating on the surface. But around these few living jellyfish there were thousands upon thousands of dead ones, flat and punctured-looking. "Killed by the oil," Thor said.

It was true, Thor said, that the voyage of the *Kon Tiki* had been across an area not sailed by any regular steamship lines, as was that of the *Ra.* Certainly that could account for some part of the new pollution. But only a part of it. "More and more," Thor said, "man is destroying the oceans on which his own life depends."

Ra I had been carried by wind and current almost to the island of Barbados. This time Thor headed deliberately for the same island. They were almost there when a storm as fierce as anything experienced on the first voyage hit them. The reed boat raced up each giant wave, then plunged down the other side like a falling elevator. With every wave they seemed on the point of sinking, and every time the vessel rose gracefully up again.

Then, without warning, there was a sudden and violent shift of wind. It struck the craft broadside and whipped the big sail around to the side before the men on watch could move. The terrific force of the wind on the sail blew *Ra II* over until one side was completely under water.

Thor was asleep in the cabin when it happened. Water rushed in over him. As he rolled out and struggled to his feet, he was waist-deep in water. But this was not a wave breaking over the paper ship. It was the surface of the ocean itself.

For the first time, both on *Ra* and *Kon Tiki,* Thor believed his craft was headed for the bottom.

Then, as suddenly as it had changed, the wind went back to its former direction. The crew, crawling along the sloping deck, fought the sail back into position. The wind lifted it. *Ra II* righted herself and sailed on.

When there was a chance to breathe again, Thor said, "That's the advantage of having a craft that floats as well on its side as on its bottom. A steel-hulled ship would never have come up again."

A few days later *Ra II* sailed into the harbor of Bridgetown, Barbados. In fifty-seven days Heyerdahl and his crew had sailed 3,270 nautical miles.

13.

A New Job to Do

WITH THE KON TIKI Thor Heyerdahl had wanted to prove that the first Polynesians might have come from America. With his reed boats he had wanted to show that the Indian legend of white and bearded men in America long before Columbus might be based on fact. He did not claim these men had come from Egypt. In his studies he had found ancient pictures of reed boats in many parts of the Mediterranean and Near East. The ancestors of Kon Tiki might have come from Crete, Phoenicia, or from a number of other places.

It was a fascinating subject for study, and Thor Heyerdahl would never lose interest in it. But his voyages on *Ra I* and *Ra II* had given him a new subject for study and work.

"When I sailed on *Ra I,* I was trying to get a glimpse into the past," he told a friend. "But I also got a glimpse into the future. And it terrified me. I saw how our modern industrial civilization is destroying itself. The real enemy of mankind is not the atom bomb. Man's real enemy is pollution of all kinds. Right now we are destroying ourselves through carelessness, waste, and greed. Unless we learn to take better care of our environment, of the world we must all live in, we will destroy that world and ourselves with it."

This is the new job to which Thor Heyerdahl has dedicated his great talents and energy. Now, living with his wife in a mountaintop home in Italy, he is widely recognized as a scientist. Scientific conventions around the world frequently invite him to speak, and everywhere he talks of the danger to human life brought on by man's thoughtlessness and greed. It is quite possible, he told one International Conference on Pollution, that within as little as twenty years man might be the victim of his own waste.

"What good is it," he asked, "for nations to fight over one or another form of government so long as we all use the ocean as a common sewer for oil and poisonous chemical wastes? Medieval man thought the seas were infinite. Modern man knows they are not. The oceans can be destroyed. And if we destroy the plankton of the oceans, we destroy all life on this planet."

Index

Ra I (Continued)
    and cameraman's ship, 85
    crew for, 75
    diver, Sourial as, 76
    doctor, Senkevich as, 76
    naming, 75
    and ocean pollution, 81
    photographer, Mauri as, 76
    sailor, Baker as, 76
    stern sagging of, 82
    trip start in Safi, 77
    trip starting problems, 79
    weather problems for, 80, 82,
        84
Ra II
    advantages of, 89
    arrival in Barbados, 91
    building, 88
    cameraman, Ohara as, 89
    carpenter, Madani as, 89
    crew, 89
    decision to build, 87
    ocean pollution and, 89
    trip of, 89
Raaby, Torstein, and *Kon Tiki*
    as crew member, 43
    as radio operator, 48
Raft, balsa
    centerboards on, 56
    constructing, 44
    ideas about, 41
Raroia reef, dangers of, 62
Reed, reeds
    boat, building, 74
    boat, crescent-shaped, build-
        ing, 72, 74
    boat, Easter Island pictures of,
        71
    boats in Peru, use of, 71

Reed *(Continued)*
    boats, trans-Atlantic possi-
        bilities of, 71
    fire and, 75
    water absorption by, 75
Reefs, dangers of, 62

Safi trip embarkations
    Ra, 77
    Ra II, 89
Scientists, theory rejection by,
    67
Sea, fascination with life of, 19
Seashell collection, 19
Senkevich, Yuri, as *Ra* doctor,
    76
Ship, crescent-shaped carved,
    32
Siblings of Heyerdahl, 17
Sourial, Georges, as *Ra* diver, 76
South American
    Indians and Polynesians, re-
        semblances between, 33, 38
    legend of white men, 71, 73
South Pacific, first interest in, 24
Statues on Fatu Hiva, stone, 32,
    33
Stone objects on Fatu Hiva, dis-
        covery of, 32
    ruins in Peru, 40
Studies
    continuation of, 69, 70
    on Fatu Hiva, plans for, 26
    of Polynesian nature, 27
    university, 23
    of zoology, 66
Swimming, fear of, 18, 28

Tahiti, first stay in, 26
Takume reef, dangers of, 62